The Barmaids of Tir na nÓg

The Barmaids of Tir na nÓg

New and Selected Poems

J.P. Bohannon

To all the Stanekers,
Best wishes in
everything —
John P Bohannon

HARROWOOD BOOKS
NEWTOWN SQUARE, PENNSYLVANIA

Requests for permission to make copies of any part of the work should be mailed to following address Permissions Department, Harrowood Books, 3943 N. Providence Rd., Newtown Square, PA 19073
eMail: harrowood@comcast.net

Library of Congress Cataloging-in-Publication Data

Bohannon, J. P.
 The barmaids of Tir na nOg : new and selected poems / J.P. Bohannon. -- 1st ed.
      p. cm.
Summary: "A collection of thirty-six poems from an American poet that reflect the experience of ancient myth, family heritage, art, science and literature in modern life. The poems range in subject from personal joy and pain to popular culture and its icons"--Provided by publisher.
 ISBN 0-915180-42-1
 I. Title.
 PS3602.O4425B37 2007
 811'.6--dc22
                              2007052770

1 2 3 4 5 '12 '11 '10 '09 '08

Text set in Horley Oldstyle
Titles set in Goudy Sans

PRINTED IN THE UNITED STATES OF AMERICA

For Michele, Moira and Bridget

Acknowledgments

Acknowledgments are due to the editors of the following publications, in which some of these poems have appeared in various forms.

Coelacanth: "To Ask You Muses once Again"; *The Irish Edition*: "To a Sad Girl, Who Used to Dance," "Elegy for an Irish Uncle," "To Martin and Debby Returning to Dublin," "Magdalene," "2/5/97: When Eight Planets appeared in the Northern Sky," "The Barmaids of Tir na nÓg"; *Oasis*: "Quartet," "Light"; *The Santa Barbara Review*: "Penelope," "Pegeen Mike," "On a Picture of Jacqueline Roque and her husband, Picasso," "The Body's Mind," "A Thing on Paper," "On the young Gabriel Garcia Marquez's being warned by a priest of an approaching cyclist"; *Verses*: "On the Church of St. Francis Assisi"

The "Dog Kennel Road" poems will appear in the anthology *Twentieth Century* to be published by Pig Iron Press in 2008.

"Penelope," "On a Picture of Jacqueline Roque and her husband, Picasso," and "Pegeen Mike" also appeared in *ART/LIFE* in a signed, limited edition of 200.

Contents

Part III

Part IV

PART I

Pegeen Mike

"I've lost the only playboy in the western world."
— The Playboy of the Western World *J. M. Synge*

The rocks of Connemara
Are a hard bed, Pegeen,
And people hereafter will talk,
Biting like salted
Wind off the screaming sea.

The colors he brought
To these grey stones and muddy turf
Were just mirage, you know,
Wispy maidens leaping and dancing,
Fleet within the blue hearth smoke.

The mind knows the truth, Pegeen
And yet the heart still lurches
Towards that jester's promise

Like a ship straining at its moorings
And pointed towards Jerusalem.

A Thing on Paper

He believed
a thing on paper
gave proof of its existence,
a love poem
fulfilled the love itself,
and a list of dreams
had surety.

She knew
essence,
a more liquid thing,
swells upward,
flows too quick to be grounded.

Paper, she said
sucks life from paint and ink,
tethers the flow of wax,
placing our dreams within the lines
like cornfields in late July.

2/5/97
When eight planets appeared in the western sky

That night, after you pointed out the planets
Aligned and visible by the crescent moon,
We sat alone. The children slept, and the silence
Between us swelled in sadness, a woeful reservoir,
Bulging with that season's tides, dammed and still.

The network news played it up, this cosmic dance,
This odd astronomy, and you asked if the sky
Was ever truly the same. Nothing is, I offered.
More accusation than answer.

Your pained eyes were like two distant stars
Foiled by the year's young moon.

The Hedgerow

Outside, the hedgerow is a cage of wooden fingers. Boxwood bushes
     asleep in December
When their deadened grayness scratches the leaden sky.

From where I sit, the three windows are eye level above the radiator
And closely crop the hedges, framed like a fairy-tale forest, a triptych of
     thorn and danger.

This year the animals have gotten in. Squirrels and mice run at night
     within the walls.
In the day the dog sniffs out the corners and frets along the floorboards.

They merely come to a warmer place, building nests within our walls.
For them there is no in or out. There is only wind or peace, the cold or
     warmth.

At night, the mice venture into the kitchen and finish off what the dog
     has left.
I sleep uneasily, listening always for the startling snap, hearing the
     intramural rustlings,

Wondering where their food is stored. Each night now, the dog must be
     locked upstairs,
Until morning when I disengage the empty traps, wary and glad there is
     nothing.

Closely the hedgerow girds the house, and within I see dark small birds
     jumping about.
In the spring I will look for the burrowing holes and block the mice and
     squirrels out.

September Dance at the Boys' School

On the playing fields behind the school,
beyond the goal posts and tackling sleds,
eleven cypress trees jut stern and black
into the croaching night.

Above the trees, a slivered moon hangs,
and Mercury, devoted, flickers white.

Three swaths of nightblue are stacked upon a strip of rust.
Sunset, mall-lights, the particulates of the evening's rush.

Before seven, young mothers
drop young children off.
Girls re-touch in rear-view mirrors,
adjust their skimpy tops, whisper behind hands
and giggle towards the gymnasium doors.

In their fathers' cars, the older ones arrive.
It is the year's first dance,
pricked alive by an early autumn frost.

On the field above the boys' school,
just beyond the towering cypress,
a boy and girl slouch tentatively,
hand in hand, into the darkness.

Light

Visitors will go on about
the quality of light in the south of France.
How fields are etched in fuzzy halos
Like cheap lamps
Atop the golden paintings
In that cellar restaurant downtown.

Perhaps, but our years together
—since they have not yet burst aflame—
Begin to glow in richer light
Grown soft with use
Like a front porch window
Awaiting me still,
When weakness has kept me away.

On the young Gabriel Garcia Marquez's
being warned by a priest of an approaching cyclist

For some reason when I imagine the scene,
he is wearing short pants. White crisp linen shorts
and then the pale, thin legs, a child's light down,
splayed glistening in the southern sun.

A thatch of thick hair, the color of coffee, crowns his head.
He looks but one way; the eyes, alert and aware
already of the world's febrile magic,
do not see this:

A mindless traveler, Quixote himself,
wheeling, unchecked, over cobbled stones.
The cycle seemed to drive the man that day.
There was no doubting that.

A priest, shuffling home from morning mass
(his almond cake wrapped in a clean white cloth,
a simple nod to the world's rich pleasures)
shouts out to the school boy stepping
into the cyclist's path.

"Mire!" (Watch out!) was all he said. And the boy,
startled, stepped back onto the curb.
The priest, laughed—it was after all a brilliant morning—
and remarked to the shaking boy:
"So now you know the power of a single word."

Gauguin

The child Gauguin saw a sketch
once of a hobo
in his mother's book.

All shadow and cross-hatching,
a formless hat and tattered coat,
strangeness, sadness and beard.

But the child also saw that joy
lifted the heavy-booted foot,
like a ministering angel
in a stranger's world.

The tramp carried a ragged bundle
tied to a stick, true to his form.

Peeling his own willow branch
there in the mother's garden,
he filled a kerchief with bread
and sand to imitate
that wanderer's pack, and
ran away from home, himself.

A small boy, some bread and sand,
a slick and whitened willow stick.

Later, when he had returned
to a mother's cold stare,
he drew his own cartoons.

Of course, he aged and married
and went into trade.

"Watch out for pictures" was all that he said
before he took off again.

The Body's Mind

(for Mary Gillespie McNeila—1907–1997)

Did those veined legs still recall the Connemara hills
Each day as she climbed the five-floor walk-up
With a netted bag of groceries and the afternoon's mail?
Could those pale eyes recall the Atlantic's pewter light
In these slanted shafts of South Bronx sun?

When she sat watching the young ones dancing
In tight embraces at a grandchild's wedding
Did she recognize then that same bursting delight
Of a high-grass meadow or that copse of birch
Along the Cliften Road by the River Erriff?

Like that other Galway barnacle, herself exiled
In a husbanded land, she too spoke her yes,
Muffled by new world scars and its strangers' ways.
Still, here, among those she loved, her cackling laughter
Pronounced the joy of a life well lived.

All this, and knowing always, (he had written in summer
That it was best now to come out), since setting off
Across the western ocean, that it all must one day wound her—
Husband, children, friends—leaving her alone.
To wait it out and to follow after.

November Stayed Warmer than Usual

November stayed warmer than usual
In these northern states
Though at night,
Without sun
We would still light a fire
To take off the chill.

When the moon was high
In a cloudless night
And white ash piled in corners of the hearth
We would trudge off to bed.
The window above us star-filled
The distance between us vast.

A Portrait of My Wife

I wake first

when the room shimmers
in dusty darkness.
Beside me
you tremble in sleep,
and snatch short breaths
like a sobbing child.

Across from us
cross the desert of bedclothes
your portrait hangs.

In this dim-lit dawn
the image seems pornographic.
The flounces of your sleeves,
your arms' odd angles
the peach in your hand
are so many limbs and breasts
and mouths.

This is my vision
of the day
as I scuttle for coffee
and the labors of morning.

Shower

Once she told me
the only moments of peace
came within the shower.

And I try to imagine.
Not the intricacies of washing,
the tired ritual of cleansing,
nor rousing visions of rivulets and tendrils,
of glistening and beaded flesh.

I see her in a cocoon of spray,
lifting her face into the water,
deciding on more, another minute or two,
forestalling the world beyond the tub,
the locked door, the whirring exhaust.

She bends her head, as in submission,
and allows the water to wash over
neck, shoulders, the arch of the back,
pounded by torrents of forgetting.

There are rare days when tears
mix with the shower's spray
just before she twists the water off
and reaches outward for a towel.

PART II

The Barmaids of Tir na nÓg

Once Ponce de Leon
searched west for unending youth.
I stop at Arch Street.

The bar Tir na nÓg—
Oirish marketry but yet
an escape before

five when young workers
pour in and fill my snug with
their noise and nonsense.

I don't share their youth.
I was old when I was young.
But here I am not.

> *Oisin himself once*
> *fell from his horse, withered and,*
> *aged out of kindness.*

> *Before time, before*
> *history, Oisin had found*
> *this land of eternal youth.*

I arrive as Man
U scores on the plasma screen.
Each Barmaid is Niamh.

NOREEN

Black-blue as raven,
her hair shines in the neon.
Richer than my pint.

Her voice is a soft
bath of vowels and elisions.
"D'ya wan tanother?"

Are my poems too
old and creaky to sing out:
"My god, what an ass"?

Last call. Our dreams she
slips in her tip jar. I leave
on the final train.

  Like Oisin, I too
  fall. I break my shoulder, and
  feel myself age there

  in front of modern
  men and women who commute
  sorely from their work.

ANNA
The only fair-haired
One of the group, she loves the
life in the USA

and keeps the church key
in the waistband of her pants.
Bottle opener.

Came out in oh-four
"The south goes to NYC
the west to Philly."

A blur of motion.
She smiles and makes me homesick
for that land of dreams.

Once in Clare, I'd drunk
at a pub two doors from her
home. She'd come to work

in America.
First one in her family
to cross the ocean.

At least in our time.
The rest stayed in County Clare
where rocks and music

bloom among burren
flowers and ancient fiddlers.
The West's awake, still.

FIONA

I'd known Fiona
before this magic evening
from a hat store way

down on Market Street.
No one was better at what
they were asked to do.

A friend's niece or else
the bride of a relation,
I remember her

as Oisin must Niamh,
even as his brittle bones
shattered on the ground

two centuries after
he last lay within her arms
and moist midnight hair.

> *There was hop clover,*
> *white clover, black medic, wood*
> *sorrel, a man with a rock*
>
> *a man with a crook.*
> *I fell out of the last train*
> *crashed, strained my shoulder.*
>
> *Modernity won.*
> *And the barmaids of Tir na nÓg*
> *dissolved into mist.*

For Martin and Debby
Returning to Dublin
after their Year in America

The adventure is always in the dream,
And even a return home
Is a journey to the world's black edge.
(But then, aren't all the great journeys
A trip back home, a longing for Ithaca,
A jaunt up that familiar stoop?)

This traveling home, this longing to leave—
All the same proud boast.
And afterwards, what remains for us?
What remains for us who stay on,
Whose stony legs sink deep in desert sand,
Is forever the stuff of grand fictions
And carousing night tales.

So now, we miss his laugh,
The North Dublin skew on life,
Its shattering morning glee.
Always the bold boy,
Striding down Chestnut Street
(As if it were a village lane and every man his friend),
He taught us to sing. Secured to the mast,
He joined in each our separate tunes.

And she—oh how I loved her
Glasgow mouth, those clipped words,
The chopped vowels like a lover's
Ragged breathing—
Her sense conjured him sane.

(But who then can ever know
what is whispered
between goddess and hero,
sailor and sorcerer,
wanderer and witch?)
In the end she protected us all.

So after it all and after it all,
It's a matter of luck wherever one lands
And something yet more when finding a home.

Two friends are now far away,
And we survive with the retelling of tales.

To a sad girl who used to dance

(For L. J.)

Pssst. Phssht. Listen. Féis.
Listen. So
        long ago, before the RIVERVISION
swelled the global banks with choral line clicks
and unison lepping, before Irishry
was every marketer's wish.

Listen.   Long before then.
She was weaving the ribbon in McGreevy's School of Dance.
An earncollade among all the Siobhans and Sheilas,
the Aislings and Marys.

"The ribbon dance" they called it.
        Simply.
Eight small ones,
        stepping in and stepping out,
                underhand and overhand,
                        weft and warp, loom and bloom.
Precise. Flowers of ribbon.
Silky weave of joy and pride.
The lighted eyes of paradise.

Oh, clap it out, my darling girl,
clap out the Sweets of May,
fairy dance, childer game,
glimmering smile. McGreevy, McGowan,
McDance, MeDance, macushla. Dance.

Hop, one, two, three, hop,
hope done, two, three, slide.

Shins splintered.
Eye turned.
Repatched, recut.
Braced. Bruised.
Heart. Earth.
Soul. Air.
Mind. Fire.

*   *   *   *   *
Dampened leaves drop
Singly into the leafy river.

"I just wanted to stop feeling so sad" you said, so thin.
Charcoaled lips, stained straw, blackened cup.
Sliding doors, shushing silence, an inner world.

*   *   *   *   *

Oh, dance again, my shimmering girl.
Leap. Clap. Dance. Turn. Wheel. Hop.

"Give us a click, girl," said Martin from Dublin.
"Up on your bike," said Willy from Cork.

("*C'est imbecile!*" You yell.)

("They are watching us still." You whisper.)

The judges, the mothers, the aunties, the others.
The trunkings of trophies, of ribbons, of medals.
Whshht! Whsssht!
Leave them. Be.
Let them. Alone.
Put them. Away.

Dance yourself, girl, in the brightening air.
Leap like the rosyfish up river
To home.
Mind it well, girl.
This leapspring, these brighteyes,
the mouthjoy, the mindwit.
They are yours. It is yours.

*   *   *   *   *

No never is it too much
for me
to dive and catch
each leafy tear
drop within the leafy river.
To catch each single leafdrop
in the teary
river. In the leafy, leaping river.

So. Dance again, my brightening girl.
Dance again once more.

An elegy for an Irish uncle

(for Tom McNeila 1924–2000)

But somehow or other I have a belief in poetry as a mystical thing,
and a dangerous thing. —Patrick Kavanagh

Well then get mystical, Paddy. I need to bury the dead.
Pieties be damned, bring on the danger,
I need to bury my dead.

So this late January morning contrives in the world's great lie
and gives us snow and sleet and steel freezing wind.
Winter weather for this marvelous man
who goat-danced in the sun, capering on the craggy cliffs of joy.

Surely, the safer path is a marshy way
where bog water seeps over boot tops,
and each squashing step, each easy squelch
damns us further— as each foot wrenches
from convention's claims to step again into the mire.

The answer, Paddy, as he well knew, is to click your heels,
high step with gleeful cackle, and steal the poetry of the sun.

"The funniest man alive," say all who knew:
say the men on boyhood corners and soldiering saloons,
in union halls and diner counters;
say sisters, cousins, the vast family sea;
say patient wife, his loyal children
who saw the laugh
and watched the fight.

Always overreaching, his was the well-told tale
over-tall and over-large—ending with a trickster's glee
and bursting through life's glimmery veil.
This was his art, his gift, his first goal of humor.

And that, Paddy is the danger:
to realize that we have missed the very moment
when this laughing man peered behind life's milky scrim
and roared to find the gods mooning all of creation.

Thoor Ballylee

At a place where salmon leap,
cattle graze and clouds drape
low on the hillside,

weather is something to be touched
and veils of sunlight hang
through the passing of an hour.

Grey stone, green pasture,
white sheep marked
with red dye and blue.

A single, twisting stretch of road from
RosMuck to Gort passes Coole and Kiltartan.
There I meet an honest man repairing
the thatch at the great poet's tower.

On a bench we sit,
he with white bread, ham,
and a flask of tea
and I with questions of technique.

The thatch itself comes from Turkey now
though copper sulfate still repels the worms.
But hooks are as likely to be plastic as hazel or birch,
though a good roof will last you some years.

Three men howl at the moon
as they walk home from Fergie's

(On a painting by Jack Yeats)

Three men howl at the moon as they walk home from Fergie's
on a slashing morning in December's cold.
(The smallest one, laughing, holds a cap in his hand,
and mouths a grin towards the sky.)
His companions, arms draped on each other's shoulders,
moan the song that a jukebox last played.
And the city is empty and nobody minds.

Three men howl at the moon as they walk home from Fergie's
and tell each other their skew and their plans.
(The smallest reveals a "can't miss" about roofing
that will keep out the heat when August goes mad.)
His companions remember a game from their youth when
a life could be won on a Saturday field
when red-cheeked young girls had looked on.

Three men howl at the moon as they walk home from Fergie's
and their breaths rise in clouds to the gods.
(The smallest one says he was married one time,
but lost touch with the woman who'd gone into the west.)
His companions recall a dance they attended,
and they elbow each other
this night and they roar.

Three men howl at the moon as they walk home from Fergie's
and they make plans to meet once again.
(The smallest one stops to get sick in the street,
wipes his mouth and runs up to his friends.)
The three turn away at 13th and Pine and walk each one alone.
The laugher snaps tight and breaks off this December
in winter's empty gray morn.

PART III

Death Pool

Just outside
Pittsburgh
houses cling to
rutted hills.

In the Evergreen
Bar you bet
on the dying.
Five dollars

a shot.
And if your man dies
before another's
the pot is yours.

So you dip
one hand
in an oily jar
pull a slip

read a name
weigh your
chances.
And the same

uneasiness
drifts down
like soot from old mills
and you tamp it slow
with beer and laughter,
lies and complaints.
And you boast

of the lives
you might
have
had.

And then
in a long week or more
when someone else's
television—singing—movie star dies,

you're back
at the jar
for another penciled name
and you wish

for once
you could
get
lucky.

Dog Kennel Road

I

For a long mile,
Dog Kennel Road twists
behind the township park.
A private road, its

potholes each spring
are filled with Quik-Patch
loosely tamped
with a spade's flat

end. It is ritual now,
this yearly conversion
of gaping, jarring pits
into the rollicking

humps
of spring.

II

In morning light,
the road shimmers grey,
dotted with mounds of asphalt,
and laced with ribbons of tar.

A fence rail,
pale and shattered,
splinters the lawn
of an old stone house,

where three deer look up,
just now.
On the porch
a man adjusts his chair

and watches
as I drive by.

III

Seven times they have gone in,
promising to stem the growing darkness,

to shatter the cumulus blackening,
like sunlight in a tired view of heaven.

In the late morning, alone, for a moment,
he sits on the open porch, eyes unbandaged

eye-drops spreading outward
across the clouded lake of his damaged lens.

What he hears is this:
the road, and a lone traveler

bouncing over pit and divot; the metallic lurch;
three deer, he counts them, bursting from the brush,

clicking against the tarmac, then nuzzling into the park;
the wind, and the slow settling of his house.

IV

Three perilous turns open upon a triptych of parkland,
follow a bubbling stream and border a ragged apron
of birch and pine and maple. All vision forward is obstructed,
bends back beyond one's destination. Along Dog Kennel Road,

the man and woman walk regularly before the coming of night.
Like some confused telling of Orpheus, she leads from behind
the man she loves, and peers back often, ear cocked for the untested
driver or the blare of youth. She touches his arm gently.

On this night, just a few feet ahead,
a rangy doe and fawn break from the deer run and
bound across the black road. Instinctively. The husband stops.
He is shaking. The two turn now and retreat to home.

There, she gathers the mail at the end of the lane
and tells him of what has been delivered.

V

In Rosetree Park, the township
drapes trees with twinkling lights
throughout the winter. Deer, in these times,
strain upward, forefeet balanced
against the bark, necks stretched taut,
and try to nibble the winking bulbs.

It is twilight and the woman moves slowly
leading her husband along the walking path.
Loose gravel scatters below their dragging feet.
"It reminds me," she says,

telling the man about the lighted trees,
"of how I've always imagined Tuscany,"

The husband adds: "But I would have guessed
The smoke of candlelight and maybe the scent of figs."

Leda in Old Age

Leda, in old age,
Bends over the evening's fire.
Rage, desire, children, all gone.
Alone she stirs the ash of memory.

One breast seared by cancer's burn,
Her smooth skin scarred by sun
An urn of eggshell, a fowler's gun,
Sit cruelly on a rough-hewn shelf.

Fear would have been too easy then,
Nesting with her clutch in bed.
Towards men (and men-like gods) instead there rose
The slick thrust of anger, the pain of knowing.

A mother's legacy, fire and death,
Floats downward slow and
Feather-like. This perversion of heaven's call,
Tonight wraps balm around her heart.

Magdalene

Perhaps because
The elders warned us
Of the danger of a woman's hair,
I see her with thick tresses,
Bush-like and black.
An olive-skinned sabra,
Her feet calloused and stained
Her eyes knowing and cynical,
She wages alone
Against what she has seen
And what she now hopes.

After all, for her, it becomes,
A decision of experience,
This new cult of proffered love.
She, who has known
The stone-edge of lust,
The oiled twist of pain,
The emptied purse of world's promise,
Races open-eyed
Into this union of joy and anguish.

Childlike once,
Magdalene now yearns for gentleness,
A revolution of perspective,
Where no lovers nail her freckled arms
Against alley walls
But speak love's agonies in
Orchards of cedar and fig.

Joan of Arc and her Angel

Just try that voices thing now, *Jeanne la pucelle*
(Though, to be honest, nobody'd bother about who the boy was,
since today we all hear our inner voices
and not just in our private hells.)

Such cosmic events are now reckoned of little worth.
Our day and time is after all,
the age of suppressed memories recalled
in shattering horror and on the unsuspecting wrought.

Now, while today angels are a trendy thing
there are few to whom your angel speaks
who turned his back on politics
and that divine mistake your vile king.

I do believe your Michael appeared far
different that those Raphaelite beauties
and New Age nymphs that modern man sees.
He'd be a simple man from a distant star.

If his descent had only come at a time less sore.
he'd have the soil of Provence under his nails,
the stink of garlic, the grit of snails
and surely would have shared some wine and more.

And that, dear girl, might have made all the difference,
won your smile and sufficed.

On a photograph of Jacqueline Roque
and her husband, Picasso, used in a GAP advertisement

The hand she raises to her throat
In seeming awe
Is a sea-wall against the tide of flurry
Bursting between the old man's fingers.

The eyes—a universe of darkness
Uncowed by celebrity
And the cleverness of men—
Bless a world
of meals and bodies
of love and compromise
of pain and blood.
      (Notice,
        Silently behind you,
      A balloon-like goddess
        Smiles and sanctions
      Your memory
Of fire
And moons
And the weight of men.
But you never tell
Him.
Indeed,
You make an odd trinity
Jacqueline Roque.
You, Picasso and that sculptured cartoon.)

We notice too
That the photographer's craft
—the magic of light rays, windows and gears—
is too sluggish to capture
that blur of creation,
too focused to define that shattering instant
When clay becomes art
When woman becomes lover
When vision joins history.

Oh Jacqueline Roque,
You who are model, wife, woman and lover
Painted, sculpted, disused, forgotten,
You have witnessed all the days of creation
And have slipped away smiling
In order to fix
The afternoon meal.

To Françoise Gilot

If that Spaniard
and the American doctor
are the comets of our age,
defining its limits, excesses and glories,
then Françoise Gilot, you are the heavens,
the ether, the sky itself
and hold universes of creation
within your being.

This stature lies
not in your bridging
the century's twin shores
of art and of science,
or in commanding
its love, in securing
its notice,

but in what you have mothered
and loved and tolerated throughout

while painting twice a thousand canvasses—
the backdrop to our age of wonder

Penelope

After he'd gone with his mad kings and heroes.
She remained woman, queen, mother.
She was no longer a wife.
The child—a worry—had come to that age
When "Why" needed an answer,
When youth tested demands.

Yet in those child fig eyes
The mother still saw
A walled-city of sadness and knowing.

How can a mother answer?
How explain the lust for battle
Or the struggle for love
To a gentle boy who climbs Ithaca's rocks,
Collects driftwood and watches the sea?

Nor is managing this pocked kingdom an easy task.
Solicitors and ministers and demi-gods
All make propositions, some less lecherous than most,

But all crash upon her like sea-foam
Upon that brace of rocks
Where last she saw sunlight
Scratch his departing sails.

The women in her court whisper
And speak of wasted youth,
The chastened moon
And the desert sands of age.
(For them, the rough beards of travelers have softened
The keening ache for soldiering husbands.)

They smile and nod as she goes daily to the loom
Where every weft and warp of vibrant thread
Weaves a net across the heart, constricts all feeling,
And gathers all memory, all hope, all desire

To be emptied,
Like the fisherman's silvery seine,
Only in the night's salted blackness.

PART IV

Quartet

(Four variations on a poem by Raymond Carver)

1.

If I were to paint a canvas filled with winter rains and minor chords,
So beautiful that your teeth would ache.
And if in twenty years you found it in a Pine Street thrift.
Would you know me and how much I love you?

2.

I dream that you are in my home.
A white room, splattered with a loaded brush of blue.
Two sofas are arranged in the parlor, alone.
Can the dream-you know
That one is enough for only us
And the other, all my life before and since?

3.

I sent you a postcard, a picture of Rodin,
White-bearded and tended by his niece.
The knobs and scars of his hands seduce the eye,
His soft hat flops towards the ridiculous,
The young girl stares vacant and unknowing.
Do you remember me and how much I love you.

4.

In my age I offer you
me as I now am
calloused and scarred
a downtown market of rags and bones
picked over, remaindered, worn.
You must remember and know I love you.

Red Peppers

Curving just so
against the palm of the hand.
Reddening
with a celestial fire
that sweats the earth itself.

This is Eden's
original fruit,
freshly-washed scarlet,
glistening, transcending
both sexes.

All buttock, all breast,
jutting with the slope of a hip,
or else phallic-formed
and bursting with seed.

To Anne Bancroft

I can still feel that moment
when Mrs. Robinson
first dropped her towel.
There was nothing revealed,
the camera pulled away too fast,
but we saw everything
there was to know.
We were sixteen.

The scene continued
 in our young minds
and into the beds
of lovers and friends,
now beyond the age
of that grinning actress
in that kind hotel.

There was such hope then
in what was reckless,
in what sent us to her
and what sent us away.
We were sandpipers
pecking at an ocean's rim
running blindly away
from the unknowable tide.

Yet there was always hope
around such danger,
the bright promise
of unsoiled love.
And in the end
she mouthed silent curses
at each of us
as we looked dumbly on.

There's not one I know
who would have left her easily,
although we knew we must.

The Church of St. Francis of Assisi – 1993

Even now,
sunlight slants through colored glass,
its broad sweep dusting the floor's
cold stone.
Rustling mice echo in the holy silence.

In a niche,
Francis, brother sun, missing hand and nose,
bespattered by iridescent birds above
smiles vacantly, a loving uncle, doddering
and put away.

Outside,
two lovers press up against the shadows—
night flowers blooming in the stone's
cool darkness,
sending roots down to the core of history.

In daylight then,
the sun—super star of its own little
system—
pierces the wafer thin heavens,
irradiating stone, color, history and love.

Handsel

(For Michele)

Handsel: (1) a gift made as a token of good wishes or luck
esp. at the beginning of a new year.
(2) a first installment

I

One must look ahead no matter.
For this arbitrary beginning
is as good a start as we are likely to get.

Sure enough these cancer cells
are last year's business,
and just as surely
will carry over into this.
As are each working man's bill
and working man's worries
—the new year's remnant
of a fleeting Christmas joy.

Still this January morning
is bright and clear
and today the bitter cold
seems cleansing and new.

II

On New Year's day
you take your morning walk,
the dog runs ahead.
The frozen leaves
form ragged hillocks,
and small baths of ice
glimmer in the path's rutted way.

Every day you tread purposefully
this same winding road,
obedient to some promise of health.
But on this early day
in the early year
you're tuned
to a doctor's recent probing
the sharpest piercing and drawing out,

done during the dying days
of the dying year.

The results, whatever their course,
will be a new year's news,
a measured and considered
extraction of fluids, cells, tissue,
a moment's work.

But just here now
where Dog Kennel Road
winds most sharply
you've learned to walk
near the edge, aware always
of the unseen car, the speeding youth
joyfully testing the freedom
of this abandoned road.

Instead,
twice today, deer break
from the brush at your side,
hurtling madly across the road,
pushed forward by the rush
of blood and desire,
much crowded by
generation, the metastasis of life,
the rivalry of survival.

III.

On New Year's Day
in Philadelphia,
a Canadian wind rattles
the Mummers'
feathery gowns.

You choose to watch on T.V.
Sound off. Just the sight
of golden and gaudy glimmer.

In the crowd that lines
Broad Street,
four deep and cheering
when the television camera pans

you see a bundled child
held high above the frozen grimaces
on a father's shoulders.

The snowsuit,
the bonnet,
the stringed mittens
run a hand
across the harp of memory
and you smile
at this new year's gift.

In the kitchen
you pour some wine
and wait
for me to come home.

She cries for no reason at all

"She cries for no reason at all," I hear on the phone.
A sister's unsure voice, trembling. And far away.

She is wrong.

I see large tears run down the side of her nose,
her throat constrict,
her lips tight because of it.

Because of a lost skate key.
A broken arm.
A shattered vase.
The slick of lamb grease
atop the stew.
Her mother. A remembered housedress.

She sees her father
(they say she was his favorite).
Feels his whiskeyed breath.
Hears his ink-stained voice.

She sees her hair in pin curls,
arms raised, crossing the line.
She was fourteen winning the 100-yard dash
on the fourth of July at Bartie's park.
She knows her smile had hope then.

Her failing body now.
Her remembered body. Sinatra in New York.
Dreams. The hats that men wore.
His going to sea. Then his going to work

And she alone and so afraid.
Her aging children.

She remembers herself,
a young girl on the front stoop
with Little Joanie—who had polio and leg braces.
How they let her play anyway
Though no one ever caught her

in their games
out of kindness.

So many houses,
so many rooms.
She rubs her temples
with her spotted hands
and tears slowly slide
down her freckled face.

On a little girl getting her hip replaced

(For Elizabeth McCafferty)

These men of science know much
and strive to perfect the flaws of god,
yet shining instruments and their steely
touch seem a heaven away
from this fairy-child who tumbled and raced
on neighboring lawns, chasing silky bubbles
and chattering a language all her own.

Picturing these serious men
folding back that freckled skin,
and wrestling with bone
is the cruel necessity of modern health,
an image not unknowable but unknown.
It seems her bird-like body
could contain no bone at all,
much less ones so twisted and sore.

Whenever we simpler, older ones
try to explain, it is always too easy
to speak of snakes in the garden
or the open wrought chest of evils and hope.
Too useless to rage at heaven and shake our fists.

For the world indeed turns with bigger ills
than the re-making of a little girl's hip.
But always such knowledge is an empty flask
and cold comfort to us who must coldly watch.

BRAINLESS

*One of his patients was a postgraduate student with an IQ of 126, a first-class
honours degree in mathematics, a regular social life and virtually no brain.
'Instead of the normal 4.5-centimetre thickness of brain tissue between the ven-
tricles and the cortical surface, there was just a thin layer of mantle measuring
a millimeter or so. His cranium is filled mainly with cerebrospinal fluid.'*
— James Hamilton-Patterson, "Do Fish Feel Pain?"
Granta: This Overheating World, No 83, Fall 2003, pp161-173.

BRAINLESS
MINDLESS
THOUGHTLESS
WITLESS
CARELESS (—or is that the heart?)
One surely would not call him DENSE.
For it is true in neither the figurative
　　　or literal sense.

Now SENSELESS is quite another fish.
That swims trumbo-esque
within the immeasurable walls of consciousness,
echoes and rattles with operatic pin-ballers
and the stale avant-garde of absurd.

(Whistle DiDi, whistle forever. Whistle while you wait.)

In Philadelphia, a band performs—Edgar Allen and the Po-ettes.
Wyrd sisters. Raving frontman. The drummer sits nude.

(I saw THE wyrd sisters once in Stratford of all places. With shaven,
shaking heads, they arrived on stage to the sound of a violin's bow across
a cymbal. There's a word for that too, you know: GRIDE as in the Shavian
scratching of nails across a slate. Don't drop yer jaws at me son, you know
well what you play.)

Tossing aside their rock, for a month before, they played
(EAP I mean now) *Hamlet* in the Brick Theater on South Street, heads to
the wall, canine monologue, accidental blood against an AC shaft
but tonight...
Again
But tonight...

the Poe-ettes sing
like graven white-goddesses,
fertile, irenic
and nurturing, oh so nurturing.

On her stony island, she sings
as the bleached bones of warrior children
clicker and clacker in the gentle toss of sea.

PAINLESS. How false.
This hurts me more.
Bullshit.
The straddled grave. It's all PAIN from the get go.
From the let go.
PUSH. BREATHE. LET GO. PUSH. BREATHE. LET GO.
It's always the pain.
"This won't hurt a bit," said Dr. Major on Chester Avenue.
(He fixed my mum's teeth when she was a girl, so long
before he wrenched away mine.)

But it did and it will and it does.
It does. And it does still.
Fail BETTER!

And so we hear
SOULLESS
POINTLESS
NEEDLESS
All deflated, sodden words.

As if the scrim of heaven
        had no purpose
        in springing free
this urban winter
or did not smile on
this fenced
dogwood tree.

A silly millimeter of brain
Matters to him. Puts him in front
        of the rest of us.

HEARTLESS
never means exactly what it says.

Ain't Nobody Looking

You know that picture
the one by Breughel
where those skinny white legs
falling from the sky
drop into the inky water
and there ain't
nobody looking.

Well, that's me.
That's my neighbors
my family, my friends,
and that simpleton
in the middle,
looking up
into the sky
like some old-world
chippicker, well
that's George W.
himself.

And doesn't it seem
how just like everybody
writes about
that musty picture
hanging there
in old world Europe?

Once, about it
Auden said that
tragedy always happens
in a small corner
when nobody's
looking.

WELL EVERYBODY WAS LOOKING!
CNN was all over the place.

In a small corner,
my ass.

There ain't no
small corners
no more.

There ain't no place
where nobody
ain't looking.

They mightn't know
that old picture
with the white boy
falling into that wine dark sea,
but they all saw those
black bodies
sea-washed
on our own
rank streets.

And they went fishing.

Don't tell me
nobody weren't looking.

To ask you Muses once again

I

To ask you Muses to sing once again is
to insult you daughters of Pieria
who have sung ceaselessly since before Olympus jutted forth,
mountaining into black heaven, soothing the breasts of men.

On the Afrique plains you first sang a river of moon-urged blood,
pulling a new world one by one from raging, ranging droves
towards fire and hearth.

There in clannish circles, midst violence and brutish pain,
the big-bellied goddess smiled upon a lambent savannah.

All belly and breast and buttock,
she knows your voices' permanence and
patiently hums with quiet sadness,
and peers into the future.

(Here, those myopic Greeks
       de-tune your song into one of venom,
       deception and evil's birthright,
       bringing your womb's fire
       to the walls of Troy, your hollowed body
       to the victor's bed.

Or

       did Creusa escape, meet sister Anna,
       travel north, travel west
       in long boats, in oaken groves?
       Bringing Dana, Danu, Bera, Brigit,
       Cerdo, Mari, Lat?)

II

Was it the soldier's hammer,
nailing the Nazarean to a tree,
that next muffled your voice?
(or the rape of a Magdalene screaming in
that masculine city of eternal sorrow?)

Then, there, still, lower, you fell, once more
        your song perpetual yet unheard.
        Wilting in the reaching-shadow of
        those rough-hewn boards.

(Softly chanted:)
        Raphael, Raphael, Raphael, angel of light,
        hear us, hear us, child, god, softly singing
        morning song in brighted Tuscany.

        Gentle birdsong, gently, faintly
        gleaned behind Portinari's smile,
        muted within the drone of cloister bells.

A rebirth? No. An afterbirth,
a painterly placenta
rich in nutritious vision
but lifeless as the marble
cocks on David,
Bacchus and the papal tombs.

Apollo, Apollo, Apollo, Apollo,
over and over, Apollo, Apollo
      (shrill, cacophonous, numbing the ears)
Days become decades, years become centuries
Apollo, Apollo, Apollo, Apollo.
      (Shrieking, discordant, pricking the skin.)
Ever and ever from hell's thick vats,
the Apollonian vision, the orphic song
that urges rugged Pluto, his catamite Mars,
—both erect, lust-blooded, muscularly formed—
to harrow the earth
to seed it with death
to harvest despair.

III

Graven faced, now,
on her bone-bleached island,
the moon-white goddess moans tunefully,
weaving pain's anguish with the tidal pulse,
the roar of blood with the heart's tattoo.
Like incense, foolish sacrifice, her moaning rises—
a salving chant, balm to the senses.
She rocks softly, endlessly, humming and scatting,
swaying and chanting. Moaning.

A single note, intoned over and over
—just above the threshold of sound—
like western snow, blankets
the cries of man.

And so you Muses, as we stumble forward, with bloated, desperate pride.
Now, after much false labor, still birth, and vengeful miscarriage—
I ask you once again to sing aloud,
to voice those spheric tones of St. Cecilia,
above the piercing wails of creation,

Give voice to those who have striven,
amidst deafening clangor
to continue to hear your song.

IV

(Chanted in recession)
Apollo's Litany:

Dresden, Bull Run, My Lai, Dunblaney, Anzio, Ypres, Belfast,
Auschwitz, Omagh, Moscow, Marengo, Rwanda, Kandahar, Watts,
El Salvador, Baghdad, Guadalcanal, Kosovo, Solomon Islands, Osage
Avenue, Wounded Knee, Alhambra, Krakow, Derry, Sarajevo,
Warsaw, Zagreb, Jerusalem, Jerusalem, Jerusalem. IRA, Red Guard,
Red Hand, Contras, UDL, RUC, Third Reich, First Republic, Aryan
Nation, 1st Crusade and 2nd Crusade, 3rd Crusade and 4th Crusade.
Jihad, Jihad, Jihad. Green Berets, Khmer Rouge, Royal Guard,
Soldiers of Fortune, Militia Men, KKK, KGB, FBI, CIA, Palermo,
Berlin, Hiroshima, Saigon, London, Paris, Tehran, Selma, Havana,
Birmingham, Beirut, Panama City, Beijing, Oklahoma, Masada,
Baghdad, Tripoli, Manhattan, Ilium,

                    and always man's heart
                    and always man's heart
                    and always man's heart.